HELPING YOURSELF
HELPING OTHERS

Dealing with SEXUAL HARASSMENT

Elizabeth Schmermund

New York

Published in 2020 by Cavendish Square Publishing, LLC
243 5th Avenue, Suite 136, New York, NY 10016

First Edition

Library of Congress Cataloging-in-Publication Data

Names: Schmermund, Elizabeth, author.
Title: Dealing with sexual harassment / Elizabeth Schmermund.
Description: New York : Cavendish Square, [2020] | Series: Helping yourself, helping others | Audience: Grades 7-12. | Includes bibliographical references and index.
Identifiers: LCCN 2019000328 (print) | LCCN 2019001272 (ebook) | ISBN 9781502646347 (ebook) | ISBN 9781502646330 (library bound) | ISBN 9781502646323 (pbk.)
Subjects: LCSH: Sex discrimination in employment--Juvenile literature. | Sexual harassment of women--Juvenile literature.
Classification: LCC HD6060 (ebook) | LCC HD6060 .S35 2020 (print) | DDC 362.88--dc23
LC record available at https://lccn.loc.gov/2019000328

Editorial Director: David McNamara
Editor: Caitlyn Miller
Copy Editor: Rebecca Rohan
Associate Art Director: Alan Sliwinski
Designer: Ginny Kemmerer
Production Coordinator: Karol Szymczuk
Photo Research: J8 Media

The photographs in this book are used by permission and through the courtesy of: :
(Note: p4, 11, 15, 18, 25, 30, 35, 39, 52, 57, 59, 67, 76, 78, 83, 89, 99; people in photos are models and the images are being used for illustrative purposes only) Cover Nito100/iStockphoto.com; p. 4 Ian Canham/Alamy Stock Photo; p. 7 Sylvain Gaboury/Patrick McMullan/Getty Images; p. 8 (background and used throughout the book) Mika Besfamilnaya/Shutterstock.com; p. 9 Steven Ferdman/Getty Images; p. 11 Fizkes/Shutterstock.com; p. 15 Shutter O/Shutterstock.com; p. 18 EvGavrilov/Shutterstock.com; p. 25 Westend61 GmbH/Alamy Stock Photo; p. 28 Richard Levine/Alamy Stock Photo; p. 30 Skynesher/E+/Getty Images; p. 35 Skynesher/iStock/Gety Images; p. 36 Mustafa Yalcin/Anadolu Agency/Getty Images; p. 39 Cavan Images/Getty Images; p. 43 Elenavolf/Shutterstock.com; p. 46 EEOC/Wikimedia Commons/File:Seal of the United States Equal Employment Opportunity Commission.svg/Public Domain; p. 48 PhotoQuest/Getty Images; p. 52 Juanmonino/iStock/Getty Images; p. 57 asiseeit/iStock/Getty Images; p. 59 Oleg Golovnev/Shutterstock.com; p. 62 Creatas/Getty Images; p. 64 Andrew Harnik/AFP/Getty Images; p. 67 Olimpik/Shutterstock.com; p. 74 Nemanjazotovic/iStockphoto.com; p.76 Garymoo/Shutterstock.com; p. 78 Daniel Tadevosyan/Shutterstock.com; p. 83 Dean Drobot/Shutterstock.com; p. 86 Tzogia Kappatou/iStockphoto.com; p. 89 Nipastock/Shutterstock.com; p. 90 Rape, Abuse & Incest National Network/Wikimedia Commons/File:RAINN logo.svg/Public Domain; p. 94 Dina Rudick/The Boston Globe/Getty Images; p. 99 VHstudio/Shutterstock.com.

Printed in the United States of America

CONTENTS

Chapter 1

Our Bodies Are Our Own

Sexual harassment is a serious topic, yet for many years American society largely ignored it. People simply didn't talk about sexual harassment that much. Victims felt scared to speak up. Abusers were able to continue to harass without punishment.

In 2006, Tarana Burke, a social activist, met a young girl named Heaven at a youth camp. Heaven was thirteen years old. One day, she asked to meet with Burke privately. There, she told Burke that she

Opposite: Too many women and girls experience sexual harassment. Recent public conversations have hopefully begun to change this.

was a victim of sexual violence. Burke didn't know what to do with this information. She told Heaven that she couldn't help her and sent her to meet with a camp counselor. Heaven left the camp and never returned, and Burke felt guilty for not being able to talk with Heaven. What she really wanted to say to Heaven was "me too." She, too, had been the victim of sexual harassment and sexual violence.

Burke used this feeling of guilt to create a movement. She created a web page about what the phrase "me too" meant to her and began campaigning to help women and girls—and especially women and girls of color—talk about and fight sexual violence via "empowerment through empathy." This means teaching women and girls that they have control over their own bodies by relating to their experiences and sharing your own. "[Me Too] is a movement to, among other things, radicalize the notion of mass healing," Burke has said. "As a community, we create a lot of space for fighting and pushing back, but not enough for connecting and healing."

Actress and activist Alyssa Milano (*left*) poses with Me Too founder Tarana Burke (*right*).

In 2017, the actress Alyssa Milano, inspired by Burke's work, wrote on Twitter that she also had been the victim of sexual violence. She included the hashtag #MeToo. Her post spread like wildfire. Soon many others—actresses, celebrities, and ordinary people—were sharing that they, too, had experienced sexual harassment or sexual abuse. Many of these

"The Weinstein Effect"

In October 2017, news outlets began reporting on sexual harassment and sexual abuse claims made against the famous film producer Harvey Weinstein. Weinstein was the most powerful person in Hollywood for many years, and he was known for making or breaking young actors' and actresses' careers. However, these news outlets began reporting that more than a dozen women gave accounts of being sexually harassed, assaulted, and even raped by Weinstein. They had never spoken out before because they were afraid of not getting any more roles in Hollywood and having their careers ruined. More and more women spoke out about how Weinstein had harassed or assaulted them. They told how he would threaten and intimidate them to never tell about what they experienced. Finally, they did. On May 25, 2018, Weinstein was charged by New York police for a sexual assault that he allegedly committed against a young actress in their jurisdiction. Other police departments also began investigating these claims.

Following his arrest, Harvey Weinstein (*center*) is taken to the Manhattan Criminal Courthouse on May 25, 2018.

As many women shared their experiences about such a powerful man in Hollywood, other people began to feel they could speak up about other powerful figures. This became known as the "Weinstein Effect." Women spoke publicly about abuse or harassment they had endured by powerful men such as Les Moonves, the head of the television network CBS, and others. Some of these incidents had occurred twenty years earlier— and the survivors only felt able to speak out about it now.

people had kept this as a secret for many years. Now, for the first time, they felt comfortable stating that they, too, had been victims.

The Me Too movement has not been just an internet sensation. It has led to real-life change. Many people who spoke out about past sexual harassment or sexual abuse—the majority of them women—have not only given attention to the fact that sexual harassment happens, but they have been able to hold harassers accountable. Many of these women demanded accountability for the people who had sexually harassed them. They demanded workplaces and schools free of sexual abuse or sexual violence. They demanded consequences for people who had committed criminal acts of sexual violence. And, for the first time in American history, their demands have begun to be met.

DEFINITIONS ARE IMPORTANT

You may have heard the terms "sexual abuse," "sexual harassment," and "sexual assault." All of these terms

Legally speaking, sexual harassment occurs in public places like offices or schools.

have somewhat different meanings, although there can be some overlap. It is important to use the most precise language possible when talking about any kind of sexual abuse or sexual harassment.

"Sexual abuse" is a term to describe any unwanted sexual behavior that one person forces upon another person. Another word to describe sexual abuse is "molestation." This term is often used to describe adults behaving in a sexual, inappropriate way toward children. Sexual abuse is criminal abuse. That means that it is a criminal act that can be prosecuted by the law.

Sexual assault is similar to sexual abuse. Oftentimes, it is used interchangeably with sexual abuse or sexual violence. As the Washington Coalition of Sexual Assault Programs states, "Sexual assault occurs when a person is forced, coerced, and/or manipulated into any unwanted sexual activity. Sexual assault is an umbrella term that includes a wide range of victimizations which may or may not involve force or be illegal."

"Sexual harassment" is another broad term. Sexual harassment is any form of bullying or coercion of a sexual nature. It does not need to include sexual touching or sexual behavior, although it can. Sexual harassment can also involve comments of a sexual nature, without any touching. Sexual harassment is illegal and can be prosecuted by the law. This term is typically used when inappropriate sexual talk or behavior happens at a person's job or school. Everyone has a right to go to school or to work without feeling threatened, and every workplace and school is legally required to protect its workers or students from such harassment.

American courts use a legal definition of sexual harassment that is a bit more involved. This definition is composed of three categories: sexual coercion, unwanted sexual attention, and gender harassment. Sexual coercion is when a person is forced to do something of a sexual nature in order to get something in return, such a better position in a job or a better grade on a test. Unwanted sexual attention means that a person focuses unwanted sexual attention on another person. Gender harassment occurs when a person makes any unwanted comments or behaves inappropriately based on another person's gender. This harassment might not be sexual in nature but rather might be based on gender discrimination. For example, a teacher who gives extra credit to male students but not female students is discriminating based on gender.

A legal term that is often linked with sexual harassment is "hostile work environment." This means that an employee's behavior creates a work environment where another employee feels that they cannot do their job correctly. This can also apply to a school. If you are in a "hostile school environment," you do not feel safe continuing your education because you are threatened by harassment. If your school or job does not take steps to make this a comfortable environment for you, then they are not in compliance with the law.

"Quid pro quo" is another legal term referring to sexual harassment. This literally means "something for something" in Latin. According to the United Nations (UN), quid pro quo occurs when "employment and/or employment decisions for an employee are based on that employees' acceptance or rejection of unwelcome sexual behavior." For example, if a boss asks an employee out one day and the employee says no, then the next day the employee is moved to a different position doing a job he or she is less interested in. The employee might assume that this occurred because they turned down the advances of their boss. This would fall under the legal definition of quid pro quo, which is a form of sexual harassment and therefore illegal.

Sexual harassment does not need to occur face-to-face; more and more, it is occurring online.

Sexual harassment can occur anywhere, although the term is often described when unwanted sexual attention occurs in the workplace or at school. However, more and more sexual harassment is occurring online. Sexual harassment does not need to occur face-to-face; in fact, it can take place in writing, on the phone, or online. If you are using a computer at work or at school to send harassing messages or to view sexually explicit material, you may be liable for sexual harassment. Sending offensive emails to your friends or colleagues can also be considered sexual harassment. For example, if you send an email to a group of people that jokes about how women are inferior, this is considered harassing behavior.

According to the UN, however, the most important part of what is defined as sexual harassment involves the term "unwelcome behavior." This UN guideline states, "Unwelcome does not mean 'involuntary.'" A victim may consent or agree to certain conduct and actively participate in it, even though it is offensive and objectionable. Therefore, sexual conduct is unwelcome whenever the person subjected to it considers it unwelcome. Whether the person was in fact accepting of a request for a date, sex-oriented comment, or joke depends on all the circumstances. This means that it doesn't matter whether or not you laugh at a sexually inappropriate joke at school, or if you agree to go on a date with a colleague that you like, who is also sexually harassing you. What matters is that these people should not behave like this to you. You have a right to not feel threatened, embarrassed, or scared at school or work.

WHAT MIGHT SEXUAL HARASSMENT LOOK LIKE?

Sexual harassment can be verbal or nonverbal. This means that it can involve spoken words or actions or gestures. It can also be physical, meaning that it involves touching.

Examples of verbal sexual harassment may include:

- Referring to a grown woman as "honey" or "babe."
- Whistling or catcalling someone.
- Telling sexual jokes or stories against someone's wishes.

Sexual harassment can occur outside in public, such as when a woman is catcalled while walking down the street.

- Asking personal questions about someone's sex life.
- Making sexual comments about what a person looks like or is wearing.
- Repeatedly asking someone out after the person has expressed that they do not want to be involved in that way.
- Telling lies or spreading rumors about a person's romantic or sexual life.
- Sending an email with an insulting sexual or gender-based joke.

Nonverbal sexual harassment includes:

- Staring at someone in a suggestive way.
- Making suggestive facial gestures such as blowing kisses or licking lips.
- Making sexually explicit signs or gestures.
- Sending sexually inappropriate pictures to people online.

Myths About Sexual Harassment

Myth: *Only women can be sexually harassed. Sexual harassment does not happen to men.*

Truth: While women are statistically more likely to be sexually harassed than men, men can also be sexually harassed. Men might also face more stigma about sexual harassment in some ways than women because it is seen as "unmanly" or something that only happens to women.

Myth: *Sexual harassment is just harmless flirting.*

Truth: There are many ways to flirt, like smiling or asking questions about how a person's day was. Sexual harassment is not flirting. Flirting occurs mutually, meaning that both parties agree to take part in flirting with one another. Sexual harassment is inappropriate behavior that is done against the wishes of the other person. Unlike harmless flirting, it can make a person feel uncomfortable and threatened.

Myth: *Women can cause sexual harassment by dressing provocatively.*

Truth: A victim of sexual harassment never causes the sexual harassment. There is nothing he or she did to cause another person to behave inappropriately toward them. A woman has control over her own body and is able to dress in the way she feels comfortable dressing. The way she dresses has no impact on whether a man will sexually harass her. Everyone is in control of their own actions toward others.

Physical sexual harassment includes:

- Touching someone when they do not want to be touched (including hugging, patting, kissing, or stroking).
- Standing close or brushing up against someone continually when they have shown the behavior is not wanted.

Any of the behavior listed above is not "normal," and it is certainly not acceptable. Yet it is sometimes accepted in our culture. Maybe you or someone you know thinks it's OK to tell a "dirty joke" at school, even if it makes the people listening feel uncomfortable. This is one of the biggest problems with combatting sexual harassment. Sexual harassment was accepted and not spoken about for a very long time. People thought that it was just something that happened that you couldn't do anything about. That attitude is changing—and it is changing all because of the brave women and men who are speaking out about their experiences.

A large survey conducted by the nonprofit organization Stop Street Violence in January 2018 shows that three out of four women, eighteen years and older, have been verbally harassed. This includes being catcalled, whistled at, or being spoken to in a sexual manner. Fifty-one percent of women reported having been sexually touched without their permission. Another 41 percent said they had experienced sexual harassment online. Men also experienced sexual harassment, although at lower percentages than women. Thirty-four percent of men reported being verbally sexually harassed, while 17 percent reported unwanted touching or sexual behavior.

The survey also asked how many people who reported being sexually harassed confronted their abuser. Women, who were most often the victims of sexual harassment, would only rarely confront their harasser. Instead, they would change their own lives so that they wouldn't run into their harassers anymore. For example, some women reported changing jobs or changing classes so that they wouldn't be around the people who harassed them. They also reported experiencing anxiety and depression after experiencing sexual harassment.

Anita Raj, the director of the Center on Gender Equity and Health at the University of California, San Diego, opened up about her own teenage daughter's experience of sexual harassment:

> **She was walking from her high school in a very privileged, affluent area, an area that most people would define as very safe. As she was walking alone around 3 o'clock in the afternoon, there was a group of boys that started calling out to her and saying things like 'nice hips.' And it just made her feel so uncomfortable [that] she didn't walk alone anymore.**

Unfortunately, this is often the case with sexual harassment. People who have been sexually harassed change their lives around so that they don't feel threatened anymore. If sexual harassment goes

If someone's behavior toward you, which is based on your gender or sexuality, ever prevents you from going to school, work, or public places like the library, that is sexual harassment.

unreported, the harassers get away without any consequence. They will most likely continue with their harassing behavior. This is why it is incredibly important to talk about sexual harassment and to take action when it occurs. That doesn't mean that reporting is always easy—or that survivors will always be listened to right away.

Eighteen-year-old Kasadi spoke with the *Huffington Post* about how she worked in a pizza shop one summer with a boy who was around her age. He always flirted with her, but she didn't respond. Then it accelerated. He would say sexual things to her and follow her home. She told her manager, who only said, "Guys will be guys, you just have to deal with it." Kasadi stated, "I didn't feel safe at work or even, eventually, at home. When I came into school every morning, I would be looking around to make sure he didn't pull his car behind me or follow me. I always hoped that it wouldn't escalate to physical assault."

Then, one day, he grabbed Kasadi in front of another coworker. The two men laughed about it. Kasadi knew that she needed to report this behavior. She told her manager what happened. He said, "Well, maybe if you flirted back with him a little, he wouldn't have felt the need to do it." No one seemed to realize what sexual harassment was or what should be done about it. Kasadi needed the money, so she kept working at the pizza shop, although she felt disgusted and scared there. Unfortunately, stories like this still occur. Survivors of sexual harassment should report the harassment, and steps should be taken legally to deal with it. This doesn't always happen, unfortunately. There are always further steps you can take, though. Sexual harassment is illegal, and it should be taken seriously.

IMPORTANT FIRST STEPS

American society is beginning to change in important ways in regard to sexual harassment. The Me Too movement has shown that sexual harassment is pervasive, which means that it happens much more than it should. For many years, people didn't talk about it. Now, both women and men are beginning to speak out about sexual harassment that occurred years previously. Media outlets are beginning to cover those important stories.

Every year, *Time* magazine dedicates its last cover before the new year to the most important person of

The final *Time* magazine cover of 2017 featured the “silence breakers,” or those who spoke out against sexual harassment and sexual assault.

that year. In 2017, it dedicated its cover to "the silence breakers"—the women and men who came out, for the first time, to break the stigma of talking about sexual harassment and sexual assault. Some of these silence breakers, like Tarana Burke, Alyssa Milano, and others, are very recognizable to us. Others are, and will remain, anonymous. Knowing their names doesn't matter as much as the importance of talking about their stories. It is in telling their stories—anonymously or not—that a public conversation can begin about how we need to stop sexual harassment and how we need to support survivors.

Chapter 2

Experiencing Sexual Harassment

When many people think of sexual harassment, they usually think of young women. This is because women are more often victims of sexual harassment than men are. (However, this doesn't mean that men cannot be—and are not—sexually harassed.) According to the American Civil Liberties Union (ACLU), anywhere from 25 percent to 85 percent of women have experienced sexual harassment in the workplace. Usually, women who are affected work in low-wage positions. They are

Opposite: Unfortunately, sexual harassment commonly occurs between teenagers at school.

especially affected in positions where they are largely paid from tips, such as waitresses in restaurants. According to Restaurant Opportunities Centers United, about 80 percent of women have reported sexual harassment at work when they work in restaurants. Because they are afraid of losing their jobs, these women usually don't speak out about the sexual harassment they have experienced.

Women of color, transgender people, and immigrants are especially susceptible to sexual harassment. According to a 2009 survey, upwards of 90 percent of immigrant women who have experienced sexual harassment have not spoken up about it because they fear the negative consequences they could face. Transgender women are particularly susceptible; double the amount of trans women report sexual harassment than their cisgender counterparts.

Men are increasingly experiencing sexual harassment, although they are less likely to report it than women. This is because they might feel insecure about reporting something that is usually seen as problem that only women experience. For example, in 2017, the Equal Employment Opportunity Commission (EEOC), reported that about 10,000 sexual harassment claims were filed. Of these, only about 17 reports were filed by men while 83 percent were reported by women. These numbers suggest that women experience sexual harassment more than men—but also that men do experience sexual harassment and might be less likely to report their experiences. In the same report, the EEOC also notes that approximately 70 percent of all sexual harassment cases are reported. That means that there are many more cases than we even know about.

These are frightening numbers. They mean that sexual harassment frequently occurs and that, oftentimes, both men and women choose not to report their experiences. So what can you do if you experience sexual harassment? How can you help a friend in need or prevent others from going through this? The best way to start is to find someone you can trust to speak to about this important issue. This person will preferably be a trusted adult, whether a member of your family or at your school. They will help you to navigate what comes next.

IDENTIFYING SEXUAL HARASSMENT

Before helping other people, however, you have to evaluate whether you have been the victim of sexual harassment. If you have ever been made to feel uncomfortable about your gender or sexuality by another person, then you may have been the victim of sexual harassment. Let's take a look at some scenarios that can happen.

Let's say that you like a guy in your class. You text and begin talking to one another in between class periods. You agree to meet for a date, but you have to cancel that day because you are sick. After that, his texts become more insistent. He states that you

If someone sends you threatening or insistent texts after you said no to going on a date, that is sexual harassment.

"owe" him another date and he is going to make sure you go out. At first, you aren't sure whether or not he is joking. You like him anyway and want to go out again. Then you get scared. One night, when you tell him you have to study for a test, he tells you that he should be more important. When you look outside of your window, you see his car there, waiting. The next day, when you tell him that you didn't like him waiting for you at your house, he only becomes more insistent that you have to go out on

The Complexities of Me Too

Actress Asia Argento has been both activist and accused in the Me Too movement.

The Me Too movement has been a powerful force against sexual harassment and sexual assault. However, that doesn't mean that the movement hasn't had its own complexities and controversies.

One of the largest controversies of the Me Too movement occurred in the summer of 2018, when actor Jimmy Bennett accused Asia Argento of sexual harassment and assault. Asia Argento, an Italian film star, was one of the most outspoken figures of the Me Too movement, and she had spoken widely about the effects of sexual harassment and assault on her life and career. Jimmy Bennett alleged that Argento had a coerced sexual relationship with him when he was seventeen years old and she was thirty-seven, after they had acted together in a film. She paid a large settlement to Bennett at the height of the Me Too movement so that he would not go public with his claims.

These claims led to troubling questions for followers of Me Too: Can an accuser also be an accused? What did this mean for the important motto in the movement to believe all survivors who come forward? Did this call the whole movement into question? But for Tarana Burke, the founder of Me Too, the claims against Argento are very much part of why the Me Too movement is so powerful. She states, “Sexual violence is about power and privilege. That doesn’t change if the perpetrator is your favorite actress, activist, or professor of any gender.” There can be all kinds of perpetrators of sexual harassment and assault. What is important is acknowledging an attack when it occurs, so that perpetrators no longer have the privilege of hiding.

a date. You begin to notice him following you both in school and outside of school. You get so scared that you tell your mom you are sick just so you don't have to go to school and see him.

This is sexual harassment. You have stated that you could not go out at certain times, and he did not take no for an answer. His behavior is becoming stalker-like. It is important that, in this scenario, you report your discomfort to a trusted adult.

Or, perhaps, you are a guy who doesn't feel comfortable yet about coming out openly in school. You know you are gay, but you are afraid of being bullied if you tell people. Then some kids in your class start teasing you and using slurs. It's very upsetting to you and interferes with your schoolwork. In fact, you tend to cut that class because you don't want to be around those kids.

This, too, is sexual harassment. It is bullying behavior, but because it is bullying focused around sexual orientation, it is sexual harassment. If the

School bullying can also become sexual harassment if it is based on sexual or gender-based jokes or innuendo.

behavior of others makes you feel so uncomfortable when you are around them that you stop going to class, that is a problem. You should speak with a trusted adult who has experience dealing with sexual harassment.

Maybe you are in a young teacher's class. He's a good teacher, and all the students like him, but he's starting to make you feel uncomfortable. After class one day, he tells you that he wants to meet with you after school to talk about your paper. You're excited that he liked what you wrote about. However, when you get to his office, no one else is there. He closes the door behind you. Instead of talking about your paper, he talks about how pretty you are and how he can't stop looking at you. You're so surprised, and you don't know what to say. Then, when you get up to leave, he gives you a hug. He says that you can be the best student in class if you just keep on meeting with him and suggests that you next meet up at a restaurant in town.

This, too, is sexual harassment. In fact, this is an example of quid pro quo sexual harassment. The teacher has power over the student because he can choose to give her a good or a not-so-good grade. When he suggests that they should keep meeting alone so that she can get a good grade, this is worrisome. He is offering a good grade in the class for one-on-one meetings of a sexual nature.

Stalking, bullying behavior based on one's gender or sexual orientation, unwanted sexual attention and touching, or unwanted sexual comments all constitute sexual harassment. Sexual harassment can also take place online or in person. It can occur via phone, via email, or via social media. If you ever feel uncomfortable with anyone's sexual comments or advances, whether online or in person, you should recognize this as sexual harassment.

NEXT STEPS

Many students or workers who are sexually harassed end up cutting school or quitting their jobs so they don't have to deal with it anymore. They might not speak to anyone about it and feel guilty, as if they caused it. It is important to realize that you are not to blame. You haven't done anything wrong. In fact, it is the sexual harasser who is completely in the wrong. Just because you are shy, or because you liked someone, does not mean that they can make you feel uncomfortable in a sexual way. It is not your fault, for example, if you flirted with a person or were so shy that you weren't firm enough when you said no.

However, it is important that you do say "no." It can be hard to say no, especially to someone you like, or someone who is older than you, or who is your boss or teacher. Nonetheless, it's very important to be clear about how you feel. Sometimes people aren't aware that what they're doing is wrong. They should know, but they may not be aware that you are uncomfortable. Maybe they aren't good at reading your body language. Whatever it is, tell them to stop. If you say no, and the behavior continues, you should write a letter to them telling them that you feel uncomfortable and that you want them to stop. You should always keep a copy of the letter for your own records.

It is important to keep a clear record of the events you experienced when documenting sexual harassment.

Record keeping is an important part of reporting sexual harassment. As soon as something happens that you think could be sexual harassment, you should write everything down as you remember it. Write it on your computer and make sure to save it where it can't be erased or jot it down in a special notebook. Include the time, the date, and the location where it happened. Write down everything that happened just as you remember it, as well as anyone else who might have seen or heard the harassment occur. You should also write down how uncomfortable it made you feel. Keep this journal in a safe place where you won't lose it or throw it out by accident. In a similarly safe place, you should also keep copies of all notes, emails, texts, or pictures the person has sent you.

In order to file a sexual harassment claim, you will need to tell a school official, like a principal or vice principal, if the harassment occurred at school. If the harassment occurred at work, you must tell a manager in order to file a claim. However, this may seem daunting. If it is too scary to talk directly with a principal or your boss, you should reach out to another trusted adult first, such as your parents, guardians, or a teacher or adult colleague with whom you are close. An adult you trust can help you navigate the rest and may even be able to approach your principal or boss for you.

Sometimes, however, when you report sexual harassment, your school or your workplace may not take action. Wait a little bit and see what happens. If you don't hear back from them and feel that your complaint was dropped, it is time to take the next steps. You should next speak with the superintendent of the school or with the owner of the company, if possible. It is also a good idea to make this complaint in writing and to keep a copy for your own records. Employers and schools who have received a sexual harassment complaint are required by law to deal with such claims by making sure that it doesn't happen again. If they do not do this, they can get in trouble with the law. However, if the head of the school or your boss at work doesn't know that sexual harassment is occurring, they cannot get in trouble with the law and have no legal duty to stop the sexual harassment. This is why it is so important that you speak out about your experiences of sexual harassment. In doing so, you can protect yourself

The US Equal Employment Opportunity Commission, or EEOC, governs workplace-related sexual harassment laws.

against sexual harassment in the future as well as any other students or coworkers who might also face sexual harassment.

In rare circumstances, after taking the above steps, you may still not feel that your complaint was addressed. Maybe you are still facing sexual harassment. In this case, it is important to escalate. Work with your parents or other trusted adults to file a government complaint against your school or workplace. If you are making a complaint against sexual harassment that took place in school, you would want to address this complaint to US Department of Education's Office of Civil Rights (OCR). If it occurred at your job, you can contact the EEOC. It is important to move onto this step quickly if you feel that your complaint to the school or to your employer was ignored. That's because there is often only a limited amount of time after the harassment occurs that you can make a complaint to the government. In the case of the OCR, you have 180 days, or about six months, to file a complaint with their office. You can write to them or call them.

The final step available to victims of sexual harassment is to file a lawsuit against the school or job where the sexual harassment occurred. This is reserved for cases where school officials or your bosses knew what happened and did not take the proper steps to prevent it from happening to you in

A Brief History of Sexual Harassment Laws in the United States

President Lyndon B. Johnson signs the Civil Rights Act of 1964 into law.

The first major sexual harassment law that was passed by the US federal government was the Civil Rights Act of 1964. This act prohibits employment discrimination based on one's race, gender, national origin, or religion.

However, the term "sexual harassment" was not coined until 1975, more than ten years later. It was in the 1970s and the 1980s that the most changes took place with regard to making sexual harassment illegal. In 1976, the US Supreme Court case *Williams v. Saxbe* established that sexual harassment could occur when a male boss made sexual advances toward a female worker. Regulations passed by the EEOC further defined sexual harassment in 1980 and explicitly stated that sexual harassment was a form of discrimination made illegal in the 1964 Civil Rights Act.

The Civil Rights Act of 1991 further regulated sexual harassment. This act expanded the rights of victims to sue if they experienced sexual discrimination and harassment, particularly at work. More important court cases followed. A particularly important one in 1998, *Burlington v. Ellerth*, stated that employers are liable for sexual harassment at their workplace if they do not take action against it.

the future. There are also strict time limits to filing lawsuits. This is called a statute of limitations. The statute of limitations in sexual harassment cases ranges from one to six years following the event of the harassment. The timeframe depends on the state in which the harassment occurred. You can look up the statute of limitations for sexual harassment cases in your state at https://www.rainn.org/state-state-guide-statutes-limitations.

All schools are required to have something called a Title IX policy. Title IX is a law that states that, "No person in the United States shall, on the basis of sex, be excluded from participation in, be denied the benefits of, or be subjected to discrimination under any education program or activity receiving federal financial assistance." This means that your school needs to provide a fair and equal educational environment for all students, regardless of their gender. If you have been the victim of sexual harassment and school officials did not take your complaint seriously, then they are in violation of

Title IX. Each school is legally required to have a Title IX officer, someone who is an expert in Title IX and makes sure that the school is compliant. You can ask your guidance counselor who the Title IX officer is for your school or your district, so that you can contact them. They can provide you with more information about sexual harassment claims and what the investigation process is like.

It is important to know that if you are a victim of sexual harassment, you are not alone. There are people who love you and who want to help you, if you can tell them about what happened. There are also many local and national organizations that offer guidance, support, education, and training in order to help sexual harassment survivors.

Chapter 3

The Effects of Sexual Harassment

Experiencing sexual harassment is devastating for everyone, no matter how old they are when it happens to them. For teens, sexual harassment can be especially life altering. It can change their faith in people they thought they could trust. It can make them doubt themselves. And it makes places that once felt safe feel dangerous and anxiety-ridden.

No matter your experience, sexual harassment is harmful to you—not only physically but emotionally

Opposite: Living through sexual harassment can be a traumatic experience, with many devastating effects.

and psychologically. Teens who experience sexual harassment at work may feel they need to give up their jobs rather than report what happened. Students who experience sexual harassment at school may be less likely to go to class or may start to withdraw from their friends. This can become even worse if the survivor of sexual harassment doesn't feel like the people they told took it seriously or listened to them. They may feel especially threatened if they have to see the person who harassed them at school or at work still.

Sexual harassment doesn't only lead to feelings of anxiety and fear, however. It can also lead to feelings of depression and anger. Many sexual harassment survivors also report feeling hopeless. In a study published in the *International Journal of Public Health* in 2017, 2,869 teens in Norway reported their experiences of nonphysical, or verbal, sexual harassment. The surveys then asked these teens about their emotional health, including experiences of "anxiety, depression, self-esteem, and body image." About 62 percent of students, both boys and girls, reported that they had experienced nonphysical sexual harassment that year. The researchers then found that these students were at a higher risk of many side effects, including anxiety, depression, poor body image, and low self-esteem. The researchers wrote, "The findings imply that although sticks and stones may break bones, it does seem that derogatory words and other forms of nonphysical sexual harassment definitely harm high school students."

Interestingly, while boys also reported experiencing verbal sexual harassment, girls were more likely to be negatively affected than boys. The study noted there were other risks that led to being more negatively affected by sexual harassment as well. These risks included "having parents who had separated or were unemployed … sexual minority status, immigrant status, and whether they had experienced physical coercion in the past year or any sexual assaults previous to that." According to the researchers, "We've found that sexual minorities generally reported more psychological distress." Usually, the people who are at the greatest risk of sexual harassment are also the least likely to report it. In order to fully tackle sexual harassment, this needs to change.

The study cited above was unique because, previously, it was thought that only physical sexual harassment was damaging. There hadn't been many studies looking into whether or not verbal sexual harassment was also psychologically damaging. The Norwegian study showed conclusively that even if there is no physical aspect to the harassment, such as unwanted touching, there can still be serious emotional impacts.

In particular, survivors of sexual harassment may experience clinical depression and post-traumatic stress disorder (PTSD). PTSD occurs after a physical or emotional shock, when our brains are trying to understand and process what happened

Many sexual harassment survivors have post-traumatic stress disorder, or PTSD, and would benefit from talking to a therapist.

to us. The name for this disorder was first coined when psychologists began studying military veterans returning from combat. It was difficult for these veterans to reintegrate into daily life. For example, they would go grocery shopping and be fearful that there were bombs on the floor that would go off. They could start having panic attacks and not be able to function doing daily tasks. However, PTSD does not just occur after experiencing the trauma of war. Other kinds of trauma, including sexual harassment and sexual assault, can cause similar reactions.

Maybe you are at the library and you think you see your harasser. Or perhaps you are in an elevator with someone who looks like your harasser. You might experience feelings of panic and fear. Your heart might beat very fast, and you might start sweating. You may change the routines of your life, or stay at home more, to avoid feeling like this. PTSD can also be accompanied by sleep disturbances and insomnia, depression, and flashbacks. Flashbacks are when you experience the traumatic moment in your life over and over again. It may feel like the event that occurred in the past is happening in the present and that you can't escape it.

Depression, anxiety, and the effects of PTSD can also create a cascade of other issues. For example, girls who experience sexual harassment are more

PTSD can cause insomnia, depression, and anxiety.

likely to participate in self-harm. They may cut themselves, for example, or drink alcohol or do drugs. Girls who experience sexual harassment are also more likely to later develop an eating disorder. Eating disorders, which include anorexia, bulimia, and overeating, allow survivors of sexual harassment to feel some control over their bodies. Oftentimes, these survivors feel like they have no control over their bodies because of what happened to them.

By controlling the amount of food they eat, or don't eat, and the way they look in extreme ways, this can help them feel like they have retaken control of their bodies—and their lives. While young women are more likely to develop eating disorders than young men, men can also develop eating disorders in response to sexual harassment or sexual violence. If an eating disorder becomes extreme, meaning that a person severely restricts the amount of food they eat, it can cause severe health problems. In fact, anorexia can lead to heart problems and even death.

Survivors of sexual harassment are at a higher risk of all of the above. Sometimes, survivors experience groups of these psychological effects. For example, depression and anxiety usually go hand-in-hand with eating disorders. Survivors with PTSD also have depression and anxiety, as well as sleep disorders such as insomnia or recurrent waking after nightmares. The effect of all of these together can be frightening. Sometimes sexual harassment is added on top of already difficult times a person is experiencing. If a person feels helpless and hopeless, and if feelings of depression are extreme, that person is more likely to take their own life. Because of these severe risks, it is very important to seek out help. Help is available for everyone, whether by seeking out a trusted friend to talk to, a counselor, or even by deciding to take anti-anxiety or antidepressant medications until you get back on your feet.

FEELINGS OF SHAME

As previously stated, most survivors of sexual harassment or sexual abuse do not come forward. This is because survivors often feel like they aren't listened to. Unfortunately, many times this is true. According to *Psychology Today*, a co-chairwoman of a government commission created to investigate sexual harassment reports said that roughly three out of four women who experience sexual harassment don't report it. Instead, according to this report, they typically "avoid the harasser, deny or downplay the gravity of the situation, or attempt to ignore, forget, or endure the behavior."

If you have been sexually harassed at school, it is important to report your experience to the principal or to the Title IX officer at your school.

Since the beginning of the Me Too Movement, we have seen many survivors of sexual harassment step forward and tell their experiences many years after they first happened. This is common. Many survivors of sexual harassment decide it is better to hide the truth, and if they ever tell about their experiences, they only report it years later. When they do come forward, there can still be a culture of "victim blaming." This means that survivors of sexual harassment are asked why it took them so long to come out if it was true. Why didn't they report it immediately? How can they remember these details so many years later?

The truth is that many survivors of sexual harassment don't come forward at the time of their harassment for many reasons. Psychologist Beverly Engel, who has spent forty years working with survivors of sexual harassment, gives several reasons for this. She states that one of the most common reasons women don't come forward after

Anita Hill and Christine Blasey Ford

In September 2018, Dr. Christine Blasey Ford claimed that the man who was appointed to be confirmed as the next Supreme Court justice, Brett Kavanaugh, had sexually assaulted her as a teenager, thirty years earlier. She provided testimony in front of the Senate Judiciary Committee, detailing her experiences and providing evidence that she had spoken about the assault numerous times over the years. She was taken to be a credible witness, and yet some people questioned why she didn't come forward years earlier. As Ford

Dr. Christine Blasey Ford testified in September 2018 about her experience of sexual assault.

herself stated, the reason was because of stigma and fear. She feared being punished for talking about her experience. Unfortunately, this was the case. Ford and her family were sent numerous threats, and they were forced to move from their home in fear of their safety. Brett Kavanaugh was confirmed to the Supreme Court later that month.

For some, Ford's testimony was reminiscent of another Supreme Court nomination in 1991. That was the year Anita Hill, a lawyer and academic, claimed that Supreme Court nominee Clarence Thomas had sexually harassed her at work. She spoke in detail about her claims, and her testimony was credible. Unfortunately, her claims were not taken seriously by members of the Senate Judiciary Committee. Clarence Thomas, like Brett Kavanaugh, was confirmed later that year. Even though Ford and Hill's claims were not fully respected, their bravery in telling their stories began an important national dialogue about sexual harassment and sexual assault.

experiencing sexual harassment is because of shame. Engel gives the example of a woman who stated she was sexually abused by Alabama politician Roy Moore when she was fourteen. That woman told the *Washington Post*, "I felt responsible. I thought I was bad." Many survivors of sexual harassment report the same feelings. Engel writes:

Time after time, clients who experienced sexual harassment at work or at school have told me things like: "I assumed it was my fault. I'm a very friendly person, and I always smiled and said hello to my boss. I think he must have thought I was flirting with him." Another client, a student who was sexually assaulted by one of her college professors told me, "I liked all the attention I was getting from him. We'd sit for hours in his office talking, and I was learning a lot from him. I guess I was sending him the wrong message."

Even though it is never the harassment survivor's fault for being harassed, many people still feel shame over the experience. This shame can prevent them from reporting what happened. They feel that they did something to cause it and so it is their fault after

Many sexual harassment survivors feel shame and blame themselves for their experience. Sexual harassment is never the victim's fault.

all. Nothing can be further from the truth. Sexual harassers harass because they can. Their behavior has nothing to do with you.

It can also feel very shameful to have to vocalize what happened to you. It is often humiliating to even think about the experience. To have to report all of the details to a boss or a principal might seem overwhelming. This is especially difficult for young women, who often have a complex relationship with their sexuality. Women's bodies are overly sexualized in American culture. This means that pictures of women, pictures focused on their bodies, are plastered across magazines and TV screens. In turn, young women are often blamed for being seen as too sexual. For example, in trials where a person is accused of rape, the women who survived the rape have often been shamed in the past.

Lawyers or investigators might ask a rape victim why she wore the short dress she did that night. Or why she decided it was a good idea to walk by herself in the dark. Or why she had a drink that night. Of course, none of these things are what caused the rape. Rape is a crime, and nothing a victim does can cause it to happen. Sadly, seeing these questions being asked of rape survivors makes young women think that they are to blame if they are victims of sexual abuse or sexual harassment.

DENIAL AND FEAR

Denial is another reason why many survivors of harassment don't come forward. Denial is tied to feelings of shame. People may feel humiliated or ashamed about what happened to them and may prefer to ignore it. They might tell themselves that they wanted it, or that it wasn't abuse or harassment. According to psychologist Beverly Engel, "As one client told me, 'I know a lot of women who were [raped], and I have friends who were sexually abused in childhood. Being sexually harassed by my boss was nothing compared to what these women went

He Said, She Said

Reporting cases of sexual harassment or sexual assault can be complicated because oftentimes cases occur without witnesses present (beyond the accuser and the accused). This is often referred to as a "he said, she said" case, where one person says that the event didn't happen and the other person says that it did. So how can investigators proceed and determine whether or not the event in question actually happened?

According to many experts, "he said, she said" is actually a myth that came about centuries ago and effectively barred women from reporting sexual assault and harassment cases. Investigators are trained to handle differing accounts. That's why they go beyond the original accounts, looking at video evidence if available and interviewing other people who might be witnesses.

They also look for corroborating evidence, or evidence that supports one side's testimony over the other's. This is a standard in investigations for any kind of crime, and it's not unique to sexual assault or sexual harassment claims. For example, if a person claims that they were sexually harassed at a conference they attended in Arizona, an early step investigators would take would be to check whether or not both people were in attendance on that particular day. They would look up plane tickets, conference tickets, and any other evidence they could find. Then, the next step would be to interview other people in attendance that day. Even if other people did not witness the harassment or assault themselves, they might give further evidence to back up the claim, such as talking about a previous case of harassment against the accused.

through. I told myself to just move on and forget the whole thing.'"

That kind of denial can lead to very complex and difficult emotions. Even if someone tells themselves that what they faced is not a big deal, subconsciously it can continue to affect and haunt them. As Engel states, "victims may experience self-doubt, which can lead to self-blame, and the hopelessness of the situation can also lead to depression." It is only in admitting that what happened was wrong and not your fault that these feelings of depression can begin to be treated.

Many people also don't come forward after experiencing sexual harassment out of fear of being punished. They feel that they will face consequences or reprisals if they report. Unfortunately, in the past, this has been the case. If a woman reported that she was sexually harassed at work, she could lose her job. However, reprisals are illegal, and there are protections in place for survivors.

Many people also don't come forward because they fear that they won't be believed. They fear that if they report what happened to them, people will think they made it up. They are fearful of being scrutinized and victim-blamed. This, too, unfortunately has often been the case. Victims of sexual harassment are often scrutinized. Unimportant and unrelated details of their lives can be brought up. Others might ask them why they said "yes" to going out with someone that they didn't trust or were fearful of. They might ask them to recall every single detail from a case of harassment that occurred years previously. If they can't remember some small details, they can be dismissed. If they do remember all of the details, they can be accused of making up the whole story. None of this means that you shouldn't report. Even with these difficulties, reporting is incredibly important. Reporting can not only stop a harasser's behavior when nothing else can, but it can also lead to healing for the survivor themselves.

REPORTING CAN HELP YOU MOVE FORWARD

There are a lot of reasons why survivors of sexual harassment might choose not to speak up. They may feel shame and fear. They may feel it's better to ignore what happened to them. But there are real consequences to not dealing with these complex emotions, and to not dealing with the harassment

It can be difficult to report an experience of sexual harassment, although it can also help you heal.

itself. People who do not confront their harassers or do not report their harasser's behavior are at a greater risk of depression, anxiety, and other psychological effects.

It's important to realize that you have value and that you, and no one else, is in control of your body. That doesn't mean that you are to blame if someone harasses you. Rather, it means that you have the right to confront and to report harassing behavior that does not take into account your control over your body.

Chapter 4

Hope and Recovery

If you or someone you know has experienced sexual harassment, it is important to reach out. If you've experienced sexual harassment yourself, talk to a trusted friend, family member, or mentor. If you think that a friend may have experienced sexual harassment, reach out to them. Being sexually harassed can be a very isolating and frightening time in someone's life. Survivors of sexual harassment may feel that they have no one to turn to for advice and no one they can trust. Their trust has been broken

Opposite: There is hope after experiencing sexual harassment.

by the behavior of the harasser, and it may take some time to rebuild.

HELPING A FRIEND

If you suspect that a friend has been sexually harassed, it is important that you express to that friend that you are there for them and will help them through it, no matter what. Your friend might tell

Reaching out to trusted family members and friends can be a lifesaver for those who have experienced sexual harassment or sexual assault.

you directly what happened. Or you may hear about something worrisome that happened from another source. It is important to approach your friend in the most supportive and nonjudgmental way possible.

If your friend tells you about sexual harassment that they experienced, the most powerful and supportive words you can respond with are "I believe you." Tell them that you believe their story and that you are there for them. It is also important to say, "You are not to blame." This is a feeling that survivors of sexual harassment often have. It can help to hear that they aren't to blame from a trusted friend, and might make it easier for them to believe themselves. The nonprofit organization RAINN provides additional prompts to help you talk to a friend who is telling you about their experience of sexual harassment or sexual assault:

- It took a lot of courage to tell me about this.
- You didn't do anything to deserve this.

- You are not alone.
- I care about you and am here to listen or help in any way I can.
- I'm so sorry that this happened to you.
- This shouldn't have happened to you.

These are helpful ways to guide you through your conversation with your friend. There are also some topics that you shouldn't focus on during your conversation with your friend:

- Don't ask "why" questions, like "Why were you alone with him?" This can be interpreted by your friend as a question that is blaming them. These details are not important to how you can be there to support your friend, so don't focus on them if at all possible.
- Don't interrupt your friend's story. Let them get it all out before you ask questions. It is important to just

listen first and to say that you are there for them, in whatever way they need. The first step of healing is to talk about the experience. You are there to listen.

- Don't judge how your friend is behaving when telling their story. A friend might be crying hysterically when they are talking. Or they might be very calm and nonchalant about what happened to them. These are both very appropriate reactions. Everyone responds to traumatic events in different ways, so don't judge or disbelieve because of the way your friend is behaving as they are telling their story.

After a friend has told you what happened, and you have listened, it is important to not ignore the topic. Keep checking in on your friend and reminding them that there is support out there if they need it. You can send them the names of local or national organizations, like RAINN, that help survivors of sexual harassment and abuse. You can suggest that they talk to a therapist or to a mentor. But don't force the issue. Ultimately, the decision is up to them. Make suggestions and, if it doesn't seem that your friend wants these suggestions, take a break and reassess. You are there as a friend, not as a professional. The most important thing you can do is to be there and listen.

You may notice that it takes longer than you expected for your friend to "get over" the experience. There is no timeframe on getting over trauma, whatever that trauma is. One person might want to deny what happened to them, and they seem to bounce back immediately. It might affect them later in their life, but as of now, it doesn't seem that it has affected them at all. That's OK. Another person, however, might take a long time to get back to "normal." They may be incredibly depressed and not feel like hanging out much. Or perhaps they do want to see you, but all they can talk about is what happened. Perhaps they don't behave like the person they once were. They get jittery around large groups of strangers. Or they don't feel like going to

It is important to support your friend who has experienced sexual harassment without judgment.

parties anymore. All of these are very normal and common responses to dealing with a trauma such as harassment. Let your friend deal with their pain in the way they need to. This may take longer than you expected. That's all right. They are on their timeframe, not yours. Try to avoid saying things like, "It's time to get over this," or "That happened a while ago. When are you going to stop talking about it?" These are not helpful comments, and they might further isolate your friend.

Instead of saying things that a friend might interpret as judgmental, remind your friend to focus on taking care of themselves. You can remind them how important self-care is. Tell them to take the time they need to get better. Encourage them to go for walks and to do things that they enjoy—and you can even volunteer to go with them. Activities like journaling, making art, and exercising are all good ways to practice self-care. You aren't there to manage your friend's health, but you can be a partner and a friend as you encourage good habits of self-care.

TRICKY SITUATIONS

Sometimes you know that something is wrong, but your friend is in denial about what happened. This is a bit of a trickier situation. For example, let's say that your friend tells you that her soccer coach told her he could take her home after practice since she didn't have another ride. On the way home, however, he stopped at a bar and took her in for a drink, even though she was underage. While they were at the bar, he kept telling her how pretty she is.

When your friend tells you this, she may not understand how serious this situation really is. She may feel special that her coach treated her like this. She may feel that it is a funny story, but you understand that it isn't.

As always, your first step is to listen and to be nonjudgmental. Don't ask your friend why she got in the car with her coach. That is not helpful. It is not her fault, and she will stop trusting you if she feels that you are blaming her in any way for what happened. Let your friend finish her story, and

Listen to friends and teammates when they try to tell you about tricky situations they've faced.

then you can say that you are worried about what happened to her because the coach should not have acted in that way. You can say, "This shouldn't have happened to you. What your coach did was wrong."

Judge what her reaction is. She might laugh you off, or she might take it seriously. If she laughs it off, you can wait until she brings it up again. Just be the good friend that you are. If she brings it up again, you can once again say that you feel the coach's behavior was wrong and that your friend might want to talk about it with her parents or with someone at school. You can provide information for local or national services for sexual harassment survivors. Provide this information slowly and delicately. Don't come on too forcefully. Your friend might be in denial about what happened to her. It is important that you give your friend the time and space they need to grapple with what happened to them in their own way. That said, if a friend comes to you and says they have been molested or assaulted, tell a parent or guidance counselor. This is not a secret you should keep.

HELP WHEN HELP IS NEEDED

Whether you are a friend who is trying to support a survivor of sexual harassment or you experienced sexual harassment yourself, you are not alone in this. There is a lot of support available for survivors of sexual harassment—whether from trusted adults and family members or specially trained therapists. The best way to find resources local to you is to start with national organizations. The largest organization that is dedicated to helping sexual harassment and sexual assault victims is RAINN. Since its foundation in 1994, RAINN has helped more than 2.7 million people. The strength of this organization is in its partnerships with over 1,000 sexual assault–service providers across the country. The organization also runs a national sexual-assault hotline, open 24 hours a day, 7 days a week, which automatically routes callers to trained staff members who work with local service providers. The hotline can provide help not only through talking to you about what happened, but by providing you with local resources and information about your local laws. RAINN also offers training and educational programs and works on public policy.

The National Sexual Violence Resource Center (NSVRC) is another large organization that aims to aid survivors of sexual harassment and sexual assault. The NSVRC provides information on their website about supporting survivors for friends and family members. It also provides guidance and support for survivors themselves. There is a large section of their website dedicated to education and prevention—information to help people learn more about the risks and harms of sexual harassment and sexual

Help is available through many organizations online.

How to Get in Touch

You can call RAINN's National Sexual Assault hotline at 1-800-656-HOPE (4673). The hotline is available all day and all night, and it's always staffed. The system works by recognizing the area code from which you are calling and routing you to a local service provider's hotline, so you can get locally relevant information. If you go to RAINN's website at https://www.rainn.org, you can

RAINN's National Sexual Assault hotline is available twenty-four hours a day, seven days a week.

also start a live chat online to talk with a trained staff member. Every talk or chat you have with a RAINN staff member is confidential, and conversations are never recorded or saved. Staff members are also available to speak with you in Spanish.

Another major hotline for survivors of sexual harassment is the Victim Connect Helpline. You can reach this helpline at 855-4-VICTIM (2846). This helpline is run through the National Center for Victims of Crime. Survivors of a wide range of crimes contact this helpline, where trained staff members are then able to direct your call to the appropriate person. The National Center for Victims of Crime offers many programs, including the Stalking Resource Center, which aims to help victims of stalking and sexual harassment in particular.

assault. Perhaps most importantly, NSVRC provides information about local resources for survivors, including networks of sexual violence crisis centers and other local support services.

Know Your IX is a relatively new organization. Founded in 2013, Know Your IX is a youth-led organization that works to end sexual harassment and sexual violence in schools. According to the organization,

> **We envision a world in which all students can pursue their civil right to education free from violence and harassment. We recognize that gender violence is both a cause of inequity and a consequence of it, and we believe that women, transgender, and gender nonconforming students will not have equality in education or opportunity until the violence ends. We draw upon the civil rights law Title IX as an alternative to the criminal legal system—one that is more just and responsive to the educational, emotional, financial, and stigmatic harms of violence.**

The organization works toward these aims by educating high school and college students about their legal rights with regard to sexual harassment and sexual violence; training and educating student-survivors to challenge their schools to work harder to combat sexual harassment and sexual violence; and advocating for changes on a local, state, and national level. Know Your IX's website includes valuable information about Title IX and other applicable laws relating to both high schools and universities, support resources, and ways to bring a chapter to your school. You can host a fundraiser for Know Your IX, bring the organization to your school for training, or start your own local chapter. This organization is unique because it is largely run and supported by students and survivors of sexual harassment and sexual assault.

Many of these organizations deal with a range of sexual harassment and violence. One organization, however, focuses completely on one aspect of sexual harassment—stalking. Being the victim of a stalker

Many people and organizations are actively working to help support victims of sexual harassment and sexual assault.

can be very frightening. You may feel that you have no safe space to go. The Stalking Resource Center provides information on its website about what stalking is and laws that are in place to prevent and fight against stalking. Their website also features a list of hotlines for victims of crime and sexual violence and tips to help survivors of stalking. The organization also provides training for individuals and organizations in how to prevent and address stalking.

There are many other organizations out there dedicated to helping survivors of sexual harassment and sexual assault. It is important to remember that support is always out there. It can be hard to reach out. Survivors often feel shame and embarrassment talking about their experiences. However, there are many people who have either been through it themselves and can guide you or who have the training to guide you through the process of reporting and, eventually, healing. Don't bear the burden all by yourself.

MOVING AHEAD

If you've been the victim of sexual harassment, it may seem like it will be impossible to move past this trauma. It is certainly hard, but it isn't impossible. Sexual trauma, as discussed earlier in this book, can provoke many unwanted consequences, including depression, anxiety, and self-harming behavior. But it is not the end

Sexual Harassment and Social Media

As our world has become more connected, the internet has become more complicated. Problems that used to occur only in person have moved online. Sexual harassment, once only a problem of the "real" world, now is a problem on the internet. Teenagers, especially, are susceptible to getting harassing sexual comments online.

Yet with increasing harassment online, there has also been an increase in fighting against online sexual harassment. The Me Too movement was able to reach millions of people instantaneously through social media platforms like Twitter, Instagram, and Facebook. A group of activists in the Me Too movement collaborated largely online by sharing information they received by anonymous sources about their harassers. They compiled large lists of people who had been accused by multiple sources of harassing behavior.

Of course, some people have said that this practice is worrisome. Anything can be shared on social media, whether it is factual or not, and people can have their reputations ruined if their information is mistakenly shared. However, social media has been a powerful tool in combatting sexual harassment and bringing people's attention to this important matter. In fact, without social media, there probably wouldn't have been a Me Too movement at all.

of your story. The best way to begin the process of healing is to acknowledge what happened to you or to someone you love. Acknowledge that it is painful and that you will need help navigating this pain and moving forward. Acknowledge that what happened to you is not your fault and that you are not able to control anyone else's behavior.

The next important step in acknowledgement is confronting the truth of what happened. If you do not feel comfortable talking to your harasser about what happened, that is fine. However, it is important to report what happened to you, either to the administrators at your school or your boss at work. This is the first step to tackling sexual harassment. And, in doing so, you are also making sure that this person will not be able to harass other people as they harassed you. If you are not immediately taken seriously, then you need to consider what other steps you can take, which are outlined earlier in this book. This may involve contacting a Title IX officer in your

While you may be fearful of the future, building a support network of trusted professionals and friends can help you recover from the aftereffects of sexual harassment.

school, or even contacting a lawyer. It is not easy, but it is a way to acknowledge that it happened to you and to state that it is not OK and that it should never happen to anyone else again.

Whatever you need to do, make sure that you have built up a support system around you, composed of people you trust. They are the ones who will help you when you feel you can't go forward. Your support system can be made up of family members, friends, and trained professionals like therapists and counselors. Remember that you are not alone in this, and that you have value and always deserve to be treated with respect.

Glossary

accountability Being held responsible.

cisgender Relating to a person who does identify with the gender given to them at birth.

coercion Persuading someone to do something against their will.

confirmed To verify; to verify someone's new position.

credible Believable.

discrimination Treating a person or group of people differently based on their sex, gender, age, race, religion, etc.

empathy The ability to share the feelings of others.

gender The social norms related to being male or female in a particular culture.

hostile Unfriendly and threatening.

nonjudgmental Not making moral judgments about a person or thing.

post-traumatic stress disorder (PTSD) A condition of consistent mental and physical stress following a traumatic experience, usually involving depression, anxiety, and sleep disturbances.

prosecution Beginning legal proceedings against someone.

quid pro quo A favor that is granted with the expectation that you will receive something in return.

scrutinized Examined closely.

stalking Harassing someone with unwanted attention.

statute of limitations The period of time when someone is allowed to bring legal action against someone else.

stigma Unfair and judgmental attitudes associated with a particular topic or person.

testimony A formal or written statement, usually given before a court of law or in front of government officials.

transgender Relating to a person who does not identify with the gender given to them at birth.

Further Information

BOOKS

Currie, Stephen. *Thinking Critically: Sexual Harassment.* San Diego: ReferencePoint Press, 2019.

Heing, Bridey. *Critical Perspectives on Sexual Harassment and Gender Violence.* New York: Enslow Publishing, 2018.

Thurston, IV. *Coping with Sexual Harassment.* New York: Rosen Publishing, 2018.

WEBSITES

FindLaw: Sexual Harassment

https://employment.findlaw.com/employment-discrimination/sexual-harassment-what-is-it.html

This website provides information about the legal definitions of sexual harassment and suggests where you can get help if you have been the victim of sexual harassment.

**Office for Civil Rights:
Sexual Harassment Resources**

https://www2.ed.gov/about/offices/list/ocr/
sexharassresources.html

The OCR website offers resources to help if you have been sexually harassed at school.

***Time*: A Brief History of Sexual Harassment in America Before Anita Hill**

http://time.com/4286575/sexual-harassment-before-anita-hill/

Time magazine offers historical information about sexual harassment in the United States.

**US Department of Education:
Title IX and Sex Discrimination**

https://www2.ed.gov/about/offices/list/ocr/docs/
tix_dis.html

Read Title IX in its entirety on this website.

US Equal Employment Opportunity Commission: Sexual Harassment

https://www.eeoc.gov/laws/types/sexual_harassment.cfm

Find resources to help people who have been sexually harassed at work.

Workplace Fairness: Sexual Harassment—Legal Standards

https://www.workplacefairness.org/sexual-harassment-legal-rights

This website provides information about sexual harassment from a legal standpoint.

VIDEOS

How the Weinstein Allegations Led to Criminal Charges

https://www.youtube.com/watch?v=ztctCII1gtY

PBS NewsHour speaks with journalist Ronan Farrow about the criminal charges against Hollywood producer Harvey Weinstein.

The Reality of Sexual Harassment I Alexandra Lindstedt I Hilliard Weaver Middle School

https://www.youtube.com/watch?v=rvvLj5ZPQns

Eighth grader Alexandra Lindstedt talks about her experiences with sexual harassment while presenting facts and statistics about this widespread problem.

Tarana Burke: Founder of the Me Too Movement on Empowering Sexual Violence Victims

https://www.youtube.com/watch?v=n6Z1KdooX-g

Tarana Burke explains why saying "me too" is a step forward for women and men who have experienced sexual harassment and sexual assault.

Bibliography

Advocates for Human Rights: Stop Violence Against Women. "Sexual Harassment." Accessed on December 22, 2018. http://www.stopvaw.org/sexual_harassment.

Cashin, Alison, and Richard Weissbourd. "Sexual Harassment Among Teens is Pervasive. Here's How Parents Can Change That." *Washington Post*, October 16, 2017. https://www.washingtonpost.com/news/parenting/wp/2017/10/16/sexual-harassment-among-teens-is-pervasive-heres-how-parents-can-help-change-it/?utm_term=.4c214834dfff.

Chapin, Angelina. "'I was Raped': 4 Teens Recall Their Own Sexual Assault and Harassment." *Huffington Post*, September 26, 2018. https://www.huffingtonpost.com/entry/i-was-raped-teens-sexual-assault-harassment_us_5babb8b9e4b091df72ecb2e0.

Chatterjee, Rhitu. "A New Survey Finds 81 Percent of Women Have Experienced Sexual Harassment." *National Public Radio*, February 21, 2018. https://www.npr.org/sections/thetwo-way/2018/02/21/587671849/a-new-survey-finds-eighty-percent-of-women-have-experienced-sexual-harassment.

Engel, Beverly. "Why Don't Victims of Sexual Harassment Come Forward Sooner?" *Psychology Today*, November 16, 2017. https://www.psychologytoday.com/us/blog/the-compassion-chronicles/201711/why-dont-victims-sexual-harassment-come-forward-sooner.

Equal Rights Advocates. "Sexual Harassment at School." Accessed on December 22, 2018. https://www.equalrights.org/legal-help/know-your-rights/sexual-harassment-at-school.

Guerra, Cristela. "Where Did 'Me Too' Come From? Activist Tarana Burke, Long Before Hashtags." *Boston Globe*, October 17, 2017. https://www.bostonglobe.com/lifestyle/2017/10/17/alyssa-milano-credits-activist-tarana-burke-with-founding-metoo-movement-years-ago/o2Jv29v6ljObkKPTPB9KGP/story.html.

Know Your Title IX. "Learn About Know Your Title IX." Accessed on December 22, 2018. https://www.knowyourix.org/about.

Stomp Out Bullying. "What Kids and Teens Can Do About Sexual Harassment." Accessed on January 1, 2019. https://www.stompoutbullying.org/get-help/teens-what-do-about-sexual-harassment.

Swenson, Haley. "That's Just One More Barrier to Coming Forward." *Slate*, September 27, 2018. https://slate.com/human-interest/2018/09/why-teenage-girls-dont-report-sexual-assault.html.

Thomas, Holly. "Asia Argento Accusations Don't Weaken #MeToo, They Show Why It's Needed." *CNN*, August 24, 2018. https://www.cnn.com/2018/08/24/opinions/asia-argento-metoo-opinion-intl/index.html.

US Department of State. "Sexual Harassment Policy." Accessed on December 22, 2018. https://www.state.gov/s/ocr/c14800.htm.

US Equal Employment Opportunity Commission. "Sexual Harassment." Accessed on December 22, 2019. https://www.eeoc.gov/laws/types/sexual_harassment.cfm.

Workplace Fairness. "Sexual Harassment - Legal Standards." Accessed on February 22, 2019. https://www.workplacefairness.org/sexual-harassment-legal-rights.

Index

Page numbers in **boldface** refer to images.

About the Author

Elizabeth Schmermund is a writer and academic. She is passionate about women's rights and working to stop sexual harassment and sexual abuse. She lives in New York with her family.